Nelson Beats The Odds
Activity Guide

Published by Creative Medicine: Healing Through Words, PO Box 2749, Tappahannock, VA, 22560

Copyright© 2018 by Creative Medicine: Healing Through Words, LLC

All rights reserved. Nelson Beats The Odds Activity Guide (including prominent characters featured in this issue), its logo and all character likeness are trademarks of Creative Medicine: Healing Through Words, LLC, unless otherwise noted. No part of this publication may be reproduced or transmitted, in any form or by any means (except for short excerpts for review purposes), electronic or mechanical, including photocopy, or any information storage and retrieval system, without permission from the publisher.

All names, events, and locales in this publication are entirely fictional.

Library of Congress Control Number: 2017901390
ISBN 978-978-099-007-7
ISBN 978-978-099-008-4

PRINTED IN THE USA

Nelson Beats The Odds Activity Guide
Written by: Ronnie Sidney, II, LCSW
Illustrated by: Traci Van Wagoner
Designed by: Kurt Keller
Contributor: Jerry Craft

Please visit www.nelsonbeatstheodds.com for information about Nelson Beats the Odds Activity Guide, Educator's Guide to the Nelson Beats the Odds Series, Rest in Peace RaShawn Reloaded, Nelson Beats the Odds, Tameka's New Dress, Nelson Beats the Odds Comic Creator app, and mix-tape. Follow us on social media and use the hashtag #RIPrashawn #TamekasNewDress, #NelsonBeatsTheOdds, #NBTO and #iBeatTheOdds. #NelsonBeatsTheOdds,

 @nelsonbeatstheo    @nelsonbeatstheo   @ronniesidneyii

 Nelson Beats The Odds
Ronnie Sidney, II, LCSW
#iBeatTheOdds

 @nelsonbeatstheo   @ronniesidneyii

Creative Medicine: Healing Through Words, LLC

CONTENTS

THE NELSON BEATS THE ODDS ACTIVITY GUIDE

Table of Contents

- **I. Coloring Pages..4**
    1. Nelson Beats the Odds
    2. Tameka's New Dress
    3. Rest In Peace Rashawn
    4. Rest In Peace Rashawn Reloaded

- **II. Comic Strip Creator...18**

- **III. Student Activities...28**
    1. How to taste a book
    2. Matching activity
    3. Somebody wanted but so then
    4. Character on a roll
    5. Character profile
    6. Word search
    7. What I think about a book
    8. Action poster

NELSON BEATS THE ODDS ACTIVITY GUIDE

INCLUDES WORK FROM

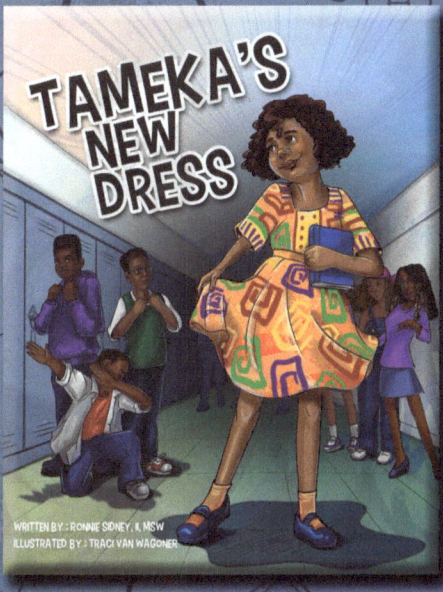
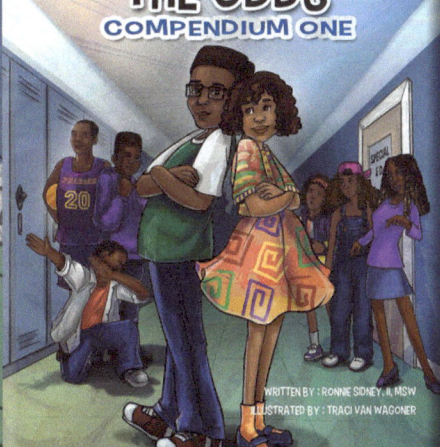

Download @ www.creative-medicine.com © 2018 Creative Medicine

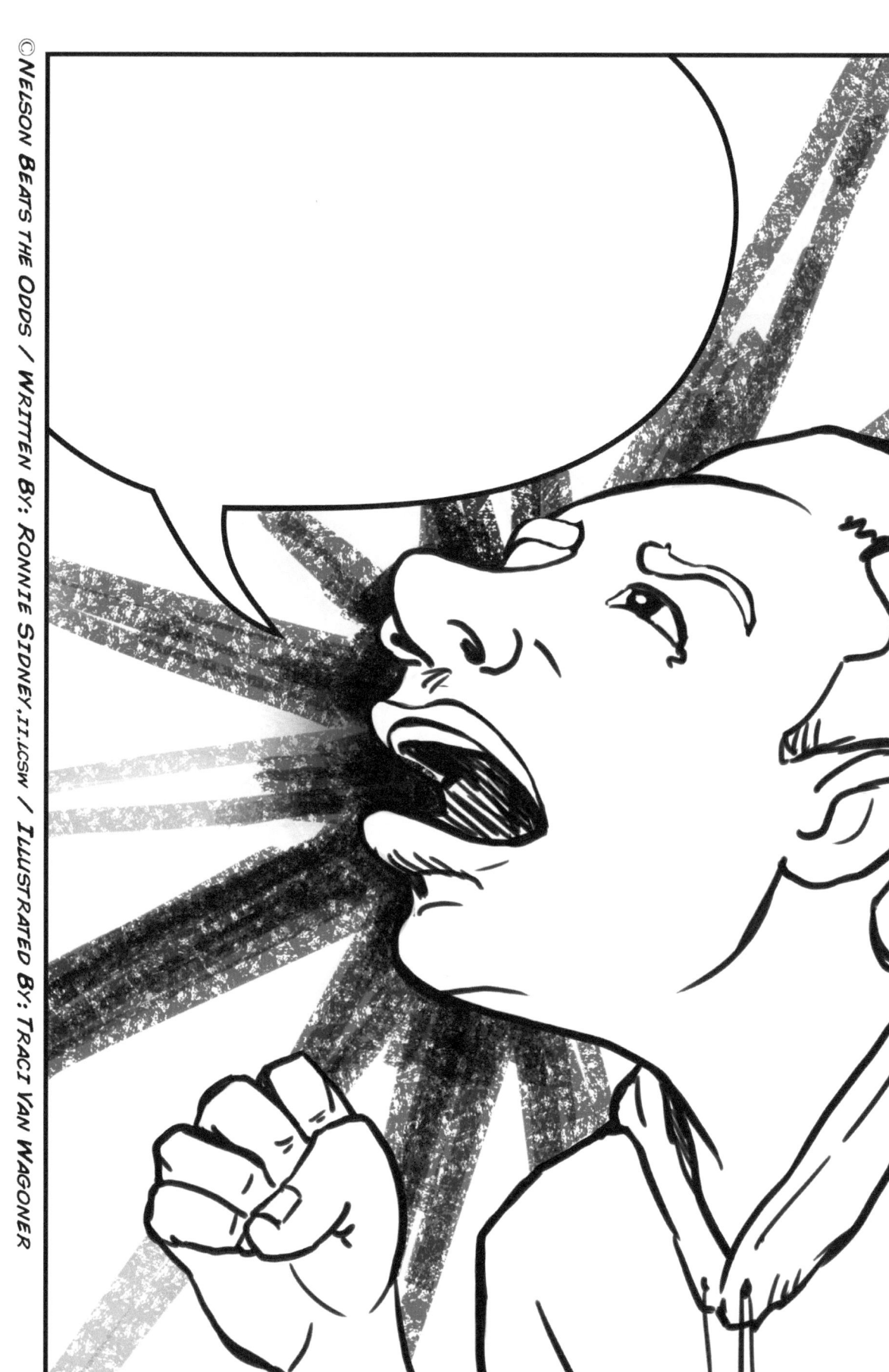

By: Jerry Craft

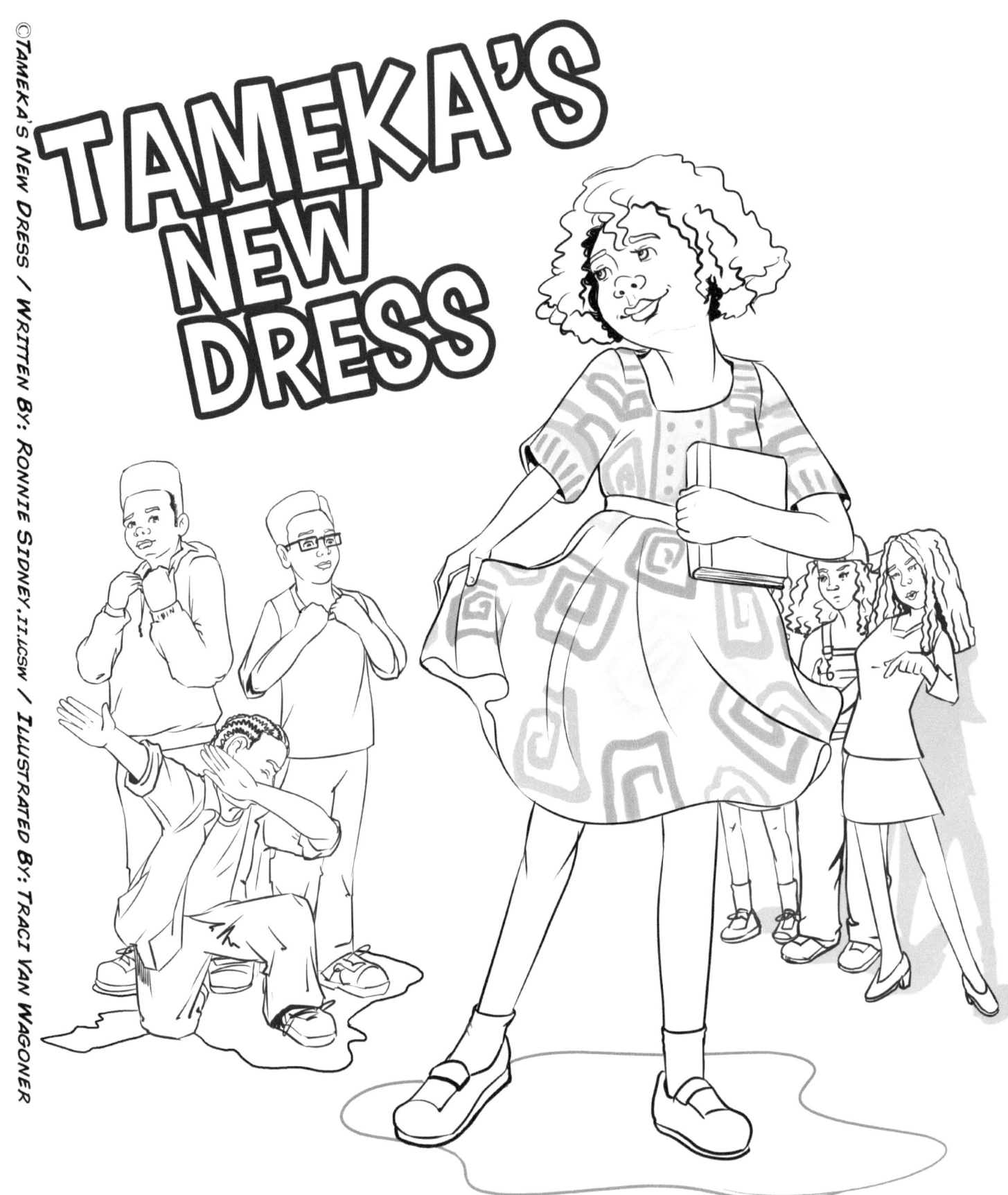

Reading Level: Grade Five

NELSON BEATS THE ODDS SERIES
COMIC STRIP CREATOR
Directions: A fun way to illustrate stories using characters, speech bubbles and text. Create a comic book story with a beginning, middle and end.

Download @ www.creative-medicine.com ©2018 Creative Medicine

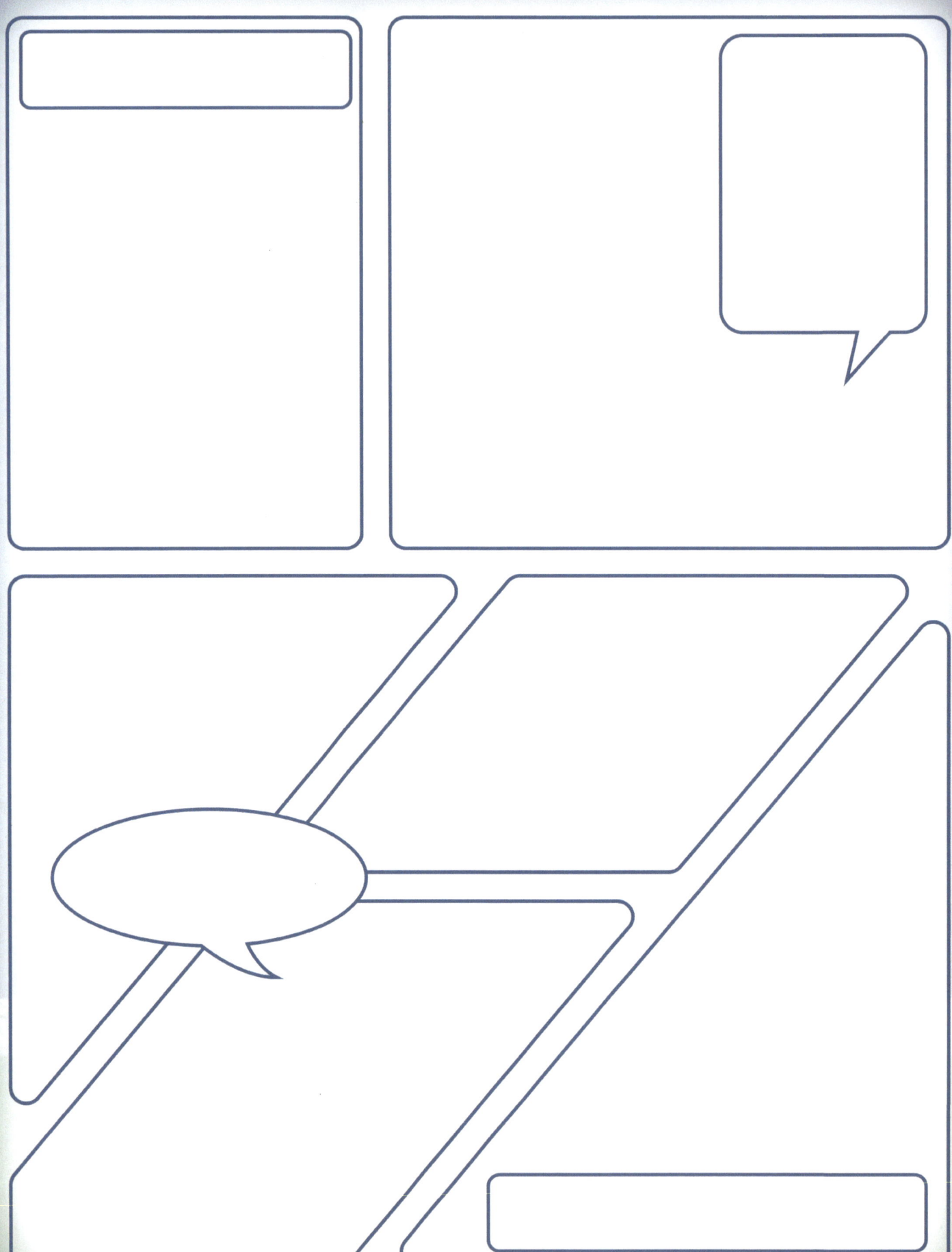

Reading Level: Grade Five

NELSON BEATS THE ODDS SERIES
SOMEBODY WANTED BUT SO THEN

Directions: After reading a book from the Nelson Beats The Odds Series, use the parses below to answer the question. Next, write a short summery of the book on the following page.

SOMEBODY → Who is the main character in this book?

WANTED → What did the character want to do or happen?

BUT → What is the problem in the story?

SO → How did the character try to solve the problem?

THEN → What was the resolution? How did the story end?

NAME: DATE: BOOK READ:

NELSON BEATS THE ODDS SERIES
SOMEBODY WANTED BUT SO THEN

NELSON BEATS THE ODDS SERIES

NAME: DATE: BOOK READ:

Reading Level: Grade Five

NELSON BEATS THE ODDS SERIES
HOW TO TASTE A BOOK

Sometimes it can be difficult to choose a book to read. Here is a list of steps you can take to choose the right book for you.
Directions: Circle the book or your choice, then complete questions 2-4. Don't forget to complete the critique below.

1 **Pick a book.** Choose up to three books for comparison.

2 **Look at front cover.** Closely review the artwork on the front cover. What's the main subject? What's in the background? Imagine what the book is about.

 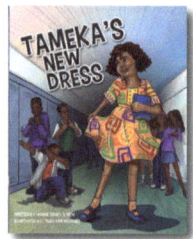 

3 **Read the back and inside flap.** This is where you find the book's summary along with information about the author/illustrator.

4 **Read the book.** Read the first 10 pages before deciding. If you got this far, you should give the book a chance. It sometimes takes a while to get into the author's voice.

What I like	What I don't like	
		Tell my friends 😊
		It's fine 😐
		Not for me ☹️

NAME:	DATE:	BOOK READ:

Download @ www.creative-medicine.com ©2018 Creative Medicine

Reading Level: Grade Five

NELSON BEATS THE ODDS SERIES
MATCHING ACTIVITY

Directions: Match the words on the right with their definitions on the left.

Self-Publishing	1	A	The view that everyone deserves equal economic, political and social rights and opportunities.
Headmaster	2	B	Not interested; indifferent.
Attention-Deficit/Hyper-Activity Disorder(ADHD)	3	C	A disorder characterized by difficulty in understanding or using spoken or written language.
Potential	4	D	A condition giving rise to difficulties in acquiring knowledge and skills to the level expected of those of the same age.
Autism	5	E	To make a humming, buzzing, or hissing sound, as an object passing swiftly through the air.
Down Syndrome	6	F	Education that is modified for those with singular needs.
Dyslexia	7	G	A genetic disorder characterized by mild to severe mental impairment, weak muscle tone, shorter stature, and a flattened facial profile.
Whizzed	8	H	A disorder of children, characterized by impaired communication, rigidity, and emotional detachment.
Learning Disability	9	I	Publication of any book without the involvement of an established publisher. The author is in control.
Special Education	10	J	A condition, usually in children, characterized by inattention, hyperactivity, and impulsiveness.
Trauma	11	K	A condition that causes trouble with written expression.
Dysgraphia	12	L	Frightening or violent events that are experienced as overwhelming.
Social Justice	13	M	The person in charge of a private school.
Disinterested	14	N	Capable of being or becoming.

Answers: 1-I, 2-M, 3-J, 4-N, 5-H, 6-G, 7-C, 8-E, 9-D, 10-F, 11-L, 12-K, 13-A, 14-B

NAME: DATE: BOOK READ:

NELSON BEATS THE ODDS SERIES
CHARACTERS ON A ROLL

Directions: Gather a pair of dice and roll them. Answer the question that corresponds to the number on the dice.

2 Where will the main character be 20 years from now?

3 How does the main character change during the story?

4 OR What did the main character do to make you dislike him/her?

5 OR How is the role of the supporting character(s) important to the story?

6 OR Cite a phrase that helps the reader learn about the main character.

7 OR What are the main character's strengths? Weaknesses?

8 OR OR What will happen to the main character in the sequel to the book?

9 OR How does the main character interact with other characters?

10 OR Compare two characters. How are they alike? Different?

11 Why would you want to be or not be the main character's friend?

12 What inspired you about the main character?

| NAME: | DATE: | BOOK READ: |

Reading Level: Grade Five

NELSON BEATS THE ODDS SERIES
CHARACTER PROFILE

Directions: After reading "Tameka's New Dress", "Nelson Beats the Odds", or "Rest in Peace RaShawn".
Select two of your favorite characters from the book and answer the following questions.

Character 1

| 1 | Book Read | Character Name | Character Gender |

What does your character do to show their personality?
_____
_____

What does your character look like on the outside?
_____
_____

What does your character say to show their personality?
_____
_____

How does your character change, or what lesson does your character learn?
_____
_____

Character 2

| 2 | Book Read | Character Name | Character Gender |

What does your character do to show their personality?
_____
_____

What does your character look like on the outside?
_____
_____

What does your character say to show their personality?
_____
_____

How does your character change, or what lesson does your character learn?
_____
_____

NAME: _____ DATE: _____ BOOK READ: _____

Download @ www.creative-medicine.com   ©2018 Creative Medicine

Reading Level: Grade Five

NELSON BEATS THE ODDS SERIES
WORD SEARCH

Directions: Find and circle all of the following words. They may be horizontally, vertically, or diagonal.

```
H R D N P D O L D F F J C A I
H B U L L Y I N G Y R W T Q M
S V K A X Y H D O T I Y E W E
A S P J F F I T A M E K A T P
G D J S S A U R D U N A M P R
Q A J T D M H A D X D B W N A
C D V E E I S U J O S C O P S
L S R R K L S M N G C D R T H
J E R E M Y G A I L H P K S A
P R V O S J L C B R O H D E W
F B Z T K S S P G I O D O U N
W I P Y D U V I A H L E R S J
K H O P E F J C C O M I C S T
X G N E L S O N G J A W T I D
T K S I X C O M M U N I T Y M
```

DISABILITY   RASHAWN   FAMILY
TRAUMA   BULLYING   COMMUNITY
TAMEKA   SCHOOL   TEAMWORK
NELSON   DRESS   STEREOTYPE
JEREMY   COMICS
HOPE   FRIENDS

NAME: DATE: BOOK READ:

Download @ www.creative-medicine.com   ©2018 Creative Medicine

Reading Level: Grade Five

NELSON BEATS THE ODDS SERIES
WHAT I THINK ABOUT A BOOK

Directions: After reading "Tameka's New Dress", "Nelson Beats the Odds", or "Rest in Peace RaShawn", answer the following questions based on the book you selected. There are no wrong answers.

1. My favorite part..._____
2. This book reminded me of..._____
3. I predict that..._____
4. I wonder why..._____
5. My favorite character is..._____
6. I was confused when..._____
7. After reading, I felt..._____
8. I was surprised when..._____
9. A part that disappointed me was..._____
10. I pictured in my head..._____
11. I like this author because..._____
12. The ending was..._____
13. The theme is..._____
14. Some evidence is..._____
15. Some words I'm not sure of are..._____

| NAME: | DATE: | BOOK READ: |

Reading Level: Grade Five

NELSON BEATS THE ODDS SERIES
ACTION POSTER

Directions: Read "Tameka's New Dress", "Nelson Beats the Odds", or "Rest in Peace RaShawn".

Create a poster that helps promote or enlighten a topic from the book.

EXAMPLES

Nelson Beats the Odds-
Learning disabilities, ADHD, stigma, friendship, and resilience.

Tameka's New Dress-
Abuse, bullying, family, substance abuse, conflict resolution, and colorism.

Rest in Peace RaShawn Reloaded-
Gangs, police involved shootings, mental health, grief, and social justice.

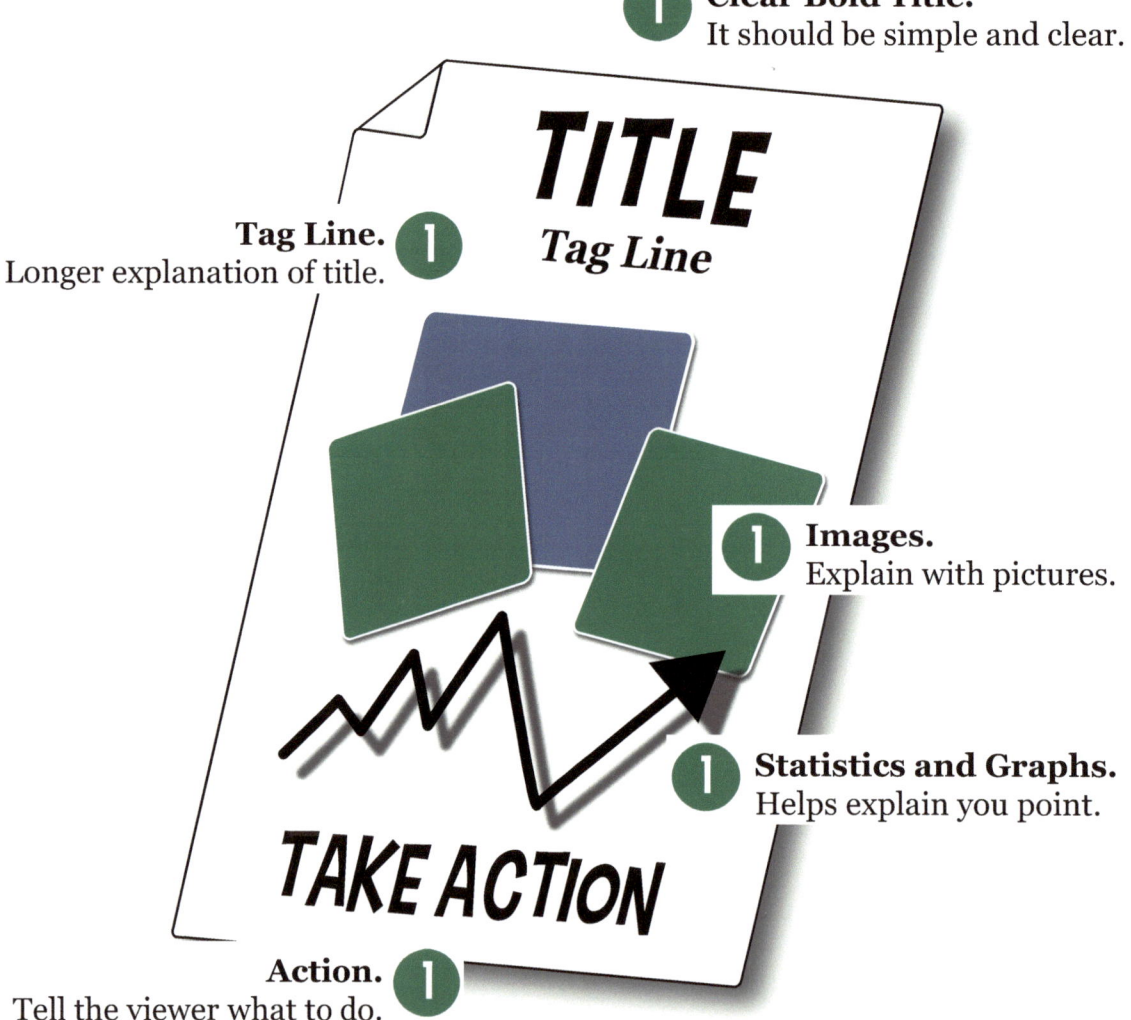

1. **Clear Bold Title.** It should be simple and clear.
1. **Tag Line.** Longer explanation of title.
1. **Images.** Explain with pictures.
1. **Statistics and Graphs.** Helps explain you point.
1. **Action.** Tell the viewer what to do.

NAME:	DATE:	BOOK READ:

Download @ www.creative-medicine.com ©2018 Creative Medicine

www.ingramcontent.com/pod-product-compliance
Lightning Source LLC
Chambersburg PA
CBHW041226040426
42444CB00002B/70